The Village Burnt By: The River Hope

The Duckling and The Tiger

"TALES OF MENTAL WELLNESS" SERIES

Vol. 1

ARLENE A. WILLIAMS

THE VILLAGE BURNT BY: THE RIVER HOPE

The Duckling and The Tiger

"Tales of Mental Wellness" Series Vol. 1

Arlene Williams

Published 2022 by

AW Publishers

Copyright © **1-11256452930**

Printed in the United States of America

ISBN-13: 979-8-9858219-0-1

Table of Contents

Dedication

The commitment that I have towards striving for mental wellness will continue to be influenced by my dearly departed mother: Leteline Brown Dell. God allowed me to care for her for three years before her passing on August 14, 2013. Mommy was only sixty-five years old, but she had a mental health condition and did not follow the treatment given to her by her psychiatrist. This, as her mental illness experiencing, told her that someone cast a *spell* on her; to destroy her. THIS WAS A LIE OF COURSE, but persons who experience delusions-false fix beliefs will have such painful thoughts. LOVE YOU FOREVER, MY MOTHER; MY FOREVER INSPIRATION TO AIM FOR MENTAL WELLNESS.

Acknowledgments

I will forever acknowledge JESUS CHRIST, MY LORD, AND SAVIOR (I Need a Savior daily). Moreover, I give thanks to my patient; **and contributor to the characters and tales in the book**, my husband: Harrington Ralph Williams, **my one and only child, who challenged me in more ways than I have time to report**: Adashia Williams; **and my three life-changing grandchildren:** Jerriya Griffin, Keyron Robinson; and Azaya Gilbert; And my **sweet sister:** Diane Elvie and her husband; my niece: and two nephews; and my brother Raphael Brown. And, my faithful auntie: Velora Sailsman in England; and my two other amazing aunties: Nellie; and Novlet; and my Uncle: Selvin Levy; and their family members at length. And, all my close cousins: especially Althea and Dorothea; and all my husband's family members at large. And, a special acknowledgement to my brother in Christ: Willie Benjamin Watts.

Disclaimer

The content of this book is inspired by the creativity that Father God gave to me on my journey thus far in life. The materials for this book is strongly influenced by the following: My work as a mental wellness counselor since 2013, the various news reports; and television shows that I have allowed into my psyche; the experiences of my friends, family members, neighbors; and my personal life experiencing extensively forward.

The Village Burnt By: The River Hope

A BRIEF INTRODUCTION INTO
THE VILLAGE BURNT BY: THE RIVER HOPE:

LEGEND HAS IT THAT IN A VILLAGE FAR, FAR AWAY NAMED BURNT, BY THE RIVER HOPE, A FRIENDSHIP EXIST, VERY UNUSUAL MUST BE STATED ABOUT THE FRIENDSHIP: A DUCKLING AND A TIGER ARE BEST FRIENDS.

LEGEND also stated that on a tough Tuesday, many, many years ago, at approximately 12 pm, a mysterious and fierce fire burned down THE VILLAGE BURNT; and LEGEND continued to state that as mysterious as the fire came, a mysterious and wild wind also came; and blew the dust and ashes of what was left of: THE THINGS, THE ANIMALS; AND THE PERSONS whom all dwell in: THE VILLAGE BURNT TO: THE RIVER HOPE.

NOW THE RIVER HOPE is described as a mystical river that's mostly filled with GOODNESS from GOD to be: CURATIVE, HEALING; THERAPEUTIC, and BEING CONTINUALLY HELPFUL.

Let us continue with THE LEGEND. LEGEND has it that no one in the: THE VILLAGE BURNT BY: THE RIVER HOPE can ever have a wrong thought for more than three minutes, without THE RIVER HOPE knowing about such bad thoughts (these to include; but not limited to PRIDE, FEAR, GUILT REJECTION, SHAME; AND MORE PAIN); and upon AWARENESS, of the bad thoughts: THE RIVER HOPE immediately bring: THE THINGS, THE ANIMALS; AND THE PERSONS into immediate care; AND MOST IMPORTANTLY INTO MENTAL WELLNESS!

Additionally, LEGEND reported that the VILLAGE BURNT settled by: THE RIVER HOPE, and the first settlers were the ANIMALS: THE DUCKLING AND THE TIGER.

The Duckling

INTRODUCTION

THE DUCKLING

The Duckling is described as Adventurous, careful, and curious at length. As one of the first animals to reside in The Village Burnt: By the River Hope, she will have lots of opportunities to pursue her inward being, which for the most part is very explorative, yet very careful and curious in many ways. This, as she will spend lots of time with her best friend forever: The Tiger.

A specific time when help was offered to the duckling, this is what the river hope reported:

THE DUCKLING

EPISODE ONE

CATCH UP ON YOUR REST
TO BE MORE ALERT AND FOCUS

The Duckling presented today with a moderate amount of sadness and with overall discouragement. Mainly, The Duckling continues to work two part-time jobs, and does not feel that she has enough energy at times to parent her two years-old and her eight months old ducklings.

Accordingly, the river ensured that The Duckling's recovery involves individual, family, and community strengths and responsibility, by utilizing a gestalt therapy concept/technique/intervention titled "ground." Briefly, this approach entails, those aspects of The Duckling's experience that tend to be out of awareness or in the background.

Immediately following, the river assisted The Duckling to identify that a major environmental stressor, situation, and or circumstance is when she has feelings of regrets due to having to work two jobs to provide for her little duckling's needs. Then, The Duckling went on to state that she will not worry about her duckling's father who resides in another country, providing for their ducklings, as she will ensure that this takes place.

Furthermore, the river continued and assisted The Duckling to implement a relaxing thought about how to be mindful on her days off from work, to catch up on her rest so that she can be more alert and focus.

THE DUCKLING

EPISODE TWO

MAKING SACRIFICES TO HAVE A BETTER LIFE EXPERIENCE IS WORTH ALL THE INCONVENIENCE YOU MAY FACE

Today, The Duckling presented with a moderate level of depressed mood; and overall anxiety. Namely, The Duckling has plans to relocate to a nearby town, and this has increased her overall stress and feelings of nervousness. To add, The Duckling will leave her two ducklings and their father behind, while she attempts to find employment and a stable residence in another town.

For this reason, the river ensured that The Duckling's recovery emerged from respect, by utilizing a reality therapy concept/technique/intervention titled, psychological need for belonging. In short, this concept consists of the needs for belonging, power, freedom, and fun; these are the forces that drive US and explain behaviors.

Immediately following, the river assisted The Duckling to identify that a major environmental stressor, situation; and or circumstance is when she engages in prolonged pondering about the negative aspects of change; instead of focusing on how changes can also bring about new opportunities.

Then, the river continued and assisted The Duckling to incorporate a distinct plan of action, to reduce her overall distress in these regards, by respectfully instructing her to make daily efforts to keep in touch with the father of her ducklings to ensure that her duckling's overall wellbeing are being addressed in a timely manner.

To this end, the river continued and assisted The Duckling to implement a relaxing thought about how making sacrifices to have a better life experiencing is worth all the inconvenience that she may face.

THE DUCKLING

EPISODE THREE

BEING MINDFUL OF USING YOUR ALREADY LEARNED COPING SKILLS

The river observed that during The Duckling's engagement in her family session, The Duckling was very nervous. Mainly, The Duckling's mother and her mother's paramour also presented and appeared very irritated with each other; and frequently yelled at each other as well.

For this reason, the river ensured that The Duckling's recovery emerged in various pathways, by utilizing a reality therapy concept/technique/intervention titled "total behaving." Briefly, this approach entails the integrated components of doing, thinking, feeling, and physiology. Choice theory assumes that all elements of behavior are interrelated.

Immediately following, The Duckling's mother expressed how bad she feels about arguing in front of The Duckling, and remarked that she will reduce this behavior. Likewise, The Duckling's mother lived in paramour reported that he will leave the home to cool off; and to which he did before this encounter with the river ended.

Furthermore, the river assisted The Duckling's mother to recognize that The Duckling's frequent displaying of defiance are being maintained in the home due to the hostility demonstrated by her caregivers. To this end, the river further assisted the duckling's mother to implement a compliance thought entailing, how being mindful to utilize the therapy coping skills programs that she has already put into place, such as the coining new words, thinking of a fruit or vegetable; and or a favorite meal; and say them quietly in her mind; and count to a specific number too simultaneously.

An example: carrots and coconuts one, carrots and coconuts two, carrots and coconuts three: AND continue onward to a specific number until a greater level of calmness; and deep breathing are attained.

THE DUCKLING

EPISODE FOUR

CORRECTION IN A RESPECTFUL MANNER
MUST BE LEARNED AND UTILIZED

The Duckling presented with a moderate about of agitation and overall sadness today. Mainly, The Duckling made a mistake at work and her manager had to correct her actions. To add, The Duckling has great concerns about her new employment, in terms of not wanting to make any more mistakes while taking orders at a pizzeria restaurant where she works as a server.

Consequently, the river ensured that The Duckling's recovery occurred in a respectful manner, by utilizing a gestalt therapy concept, titled, "introjection." Briefly, this concept/technique/intervention entails the uncritical acceptance of others' beliefs and standards without assimilating them into one's own personality.

Immediately following, the river guided The Duckling to identify that a major environmental stressor, situation, and or circumstance is when she feels that if she makes mistakes while learning a new skill, she is not smart enough. Indeed, The Duckling stated that she was happy for her manager's corrections, as he was very nice about the way he pointed out her mistakes. Certainly, the river further assisted The Duckling to implement a relaxing thought about how when she is corrected in a respectful manner, she will learn how to approach other persons likewise when she perceives she has been treated badly by them in many ways.

THE DUCKLING

EPISODE FIVE

THE NEED TO INTERACT WITH FAMILY MEMBERS SO THEY CAN KNOW YOU BETTER; AND LIKEWISE YOU CAN KNOW THEM BETTER

The Duckling presented today for her family session with an elevated level of cooperation; and overall pleasantness. However, The Duckling's mother also presented and elaborately reported how The Duckling continues to isolate herself inside her room and engaged in prolonged playing on her video games.

Consequently, the river ensured that The Duckling's recovery emerged in a holistic manner, by utilizing a reality therapy concept/technique/intervention titled "total behaving." Briefly speaking, this approach entails, the integrated components of doing, thinking, feeling, and physiology. Choice theory assumes that all elements of behavior are interrelated.

Immediately thereafter, the river assisted The Duckling to identify that a major environmental stressor, situation, and or circumstance is when she does not make time to communicate with her family members, and thus create a home environment of great discord. Then, The Duckling stated that she oftentimes comes out of her room to do a quick check on her mother and younger sister, and then return to her private area within her room. Furthermore, the river continued and assisted The Duckling to implement a relaxing thought about how she need to interact with her family members so that she can get to know them better; and they likewise can know her better too.

THE DUCKLING

EPISODE SIX

HAVING PEOPLE CLOSE BY WHO CARES ABOUT YOU; CAN REDUCE YOUR STRESS LEVEL IN MANY WAYS

The Duckling presented with a moderate amount of agitation and overall with feelings of sadness. Briefly, The Duckling's husband was driving in their family car yesterday, and another driver hit their vehicle in the rear; and drove off. To add, The Duckling is tired as she and her husband went to the hospital during the night and she did not get enough sleep.

Certainly, the river ensured that The Duckling's recovery emerged from respect, by utilizing a gestalt therapy concept/technique/intervention titled "ground."

Briefly, this approach involves those aspects of the individual's experience that tend to be out of awareness or in the background.

Immediately after, the river coached The Duckling to identify that a major environmental stressor, situation, and or circumstance is when she does not considerate for a longer time how fortunate she is that she was not hurt during the car accident; and likewise her husband. Furthermore, The Duckling remarked that she is happy that she has the support of her older sister, who is currently residing with her, as she has plans to catch up on her rest without worrying about her children and the household tasks. Furthermore, the river continued and motivated The Duckling to implement a relaxing thought about how having people close by who care about her, can reduce her overall stress level in many ways.

THE DUCKLING

EPISODE SEVEN

BEING CARED FOR CAN HELP PERSONS TO LEARN MANY THINGS, AND BE SMARTER TOO

The Duckling presented with a moderate amount of agitation and overall with sadness in her affect; and speech as well. Briefly speaking, The Duckling's telephone is broken as she threw it on the side of a wall in her current residence. This, as The Duckling did not want her grandmother to tell her to turn off the light and go to bed.

Consequently, the river ensured that The Duckling's recovery emerged in holistic manner, by utilizing a reality therapy concept titled psychological need for fun. Namely, this concept/technique/intervention entails the needs for belonging, power, freedom, and fun; these are the forces that drive humans and explain behavior.

Furthermore, the river supported The Duckling to identify that a major environmental stressor, situation, and or circumstance is when she does not understand that her fun must stop so that she can be more rested to have more fun. At length, The Duckling remarked that so many people are correcting her behaviors; and she feels that they love her, but it also gets on her nerves as well. Indeed, the river continued and directed

The Duckling to implement a relaxing thought about how if she was not cared about, she will not learn so many things; and be as smart as she is now.

The Tiger

INTRODUCTION

THE TIGER

The Tiger is described as Serious, stable, and very thoughtful. As the very first animal to step paws on The Village Burnt By: The River Hope, he will ensure that he pursues all his relationships with a sense of importance, determination, and being very mindful of all his moves; especially with The Duckling.

A specific time when help was offered to the tiger, this is what the river reported:

THE TIGER

EPISODE ONE

IMITATING THE THINGS, ANIMALS, AND GOOD PERSONS

Today, this river hope ensured that The Tiger's recovery happened in a holistic manner. Overall, this tiger appeared tired; and with feelings of helplessness throughout his time with the river; but he strived to engage with the river hope. Onward, The Tiger's mother presented and greatly reported that she and The Tiger had a very busy week, as they attended to different family matters within their community. And, while this tiger's mother talked with lots of things, animals; and people within the community involving:

The Village Burnt By: The River Hope; with a high level of courtesy, The Tiger viewed the displayed of courtesy by his mother as being quite annoying for an extended time. Namely, as this tiger truly devalues when social gatherings with others demand that he has a better attitude for a longer time.

Additionally forward, the river assisted The Tiger to identify that a major environmental stressor, situation, and or circumstance is when he does not understand that there are a lot of important things in life; and one of them is being respectful and kind to others in many ways.

Afterwards, The Tiger stated he is glad that his mother took him and his brother to her boyfriend's house; as the boyfriend has an exercise machine that The Tiger likes.

Moving forward in this respect, the river hope continued and further inspired this tiger to implement a relaxing thought, by extensively discussing with The Tiger about how noticing the good behaviors of the things, the animals; and the persons, such as his mother, should be more appreciated and copied by him for many more days.

THE TIGER

EPISODE TWO

HANDLING FEELINGS OF DISAPPOINTMENTS

Today, The Tiger presented with an elevated amount of sadness and overall with feeling of frustration too. Mainly, The Tiger has not heard from his father in a couple of weeks and has great concerns; and overall worried that his father may not be well. To be more precise, The Tiger believes that his father is abusing drugs, and does not want to let him know about it. To add, The Tiger did not get a pair of shoes that his father promised, and The Tiger has contributed this to the fact that this is his father's past behaving when he is using various illegal substances.

Consequently, the river ensured that The Tiger's recovery emerged from hope, by utilizing a reality therapy concept/technique, titled "paining behavior."

In short, this approach entails, choosing misery by developing symptoms (such as head aching, depressing, and anxietying) because these seem like the best behaviors available at the time.

Immediately thereafter, the river assisted The Tiger to identify that a major environmental stressor, situation, and or circumstance is when he ponders extensively about a possible feared activity or event without knowing if these are truly the right thinking to apply in such cases.

Consequently, The Tiger positively stated that he wants to call his father and find out how he is doing; and will obtain his father's number from one of his caring caregivers. Moreover, the river continued and further assisted The Tiger to implement a relaxing thought by encouraging him to write a short paragraph about his feelings of disappointments; so that he can get such bad thinking out of his head; and put them on a sheet of paper instead.

THE TIGER

EPISODE THREE

REMEMBERING GOOD HEALTH FROM THE PAST WHEN NEW AND CHALLENGING HEALTH ISSUES ARISE IN THE PRESENT

Mainly, The Tiger went to the ophthalmologist and was informed that he has glaucoma. To add, The Tiger primary care doctor placed The Tiger on medication for hypertension and these have both increased The Tiger's level of distress.

Consequently, the river ensured that The Tiger's recovery emerged in a holistic manner, by utilizing a gestalt therapy concept/technique, titled, "introjection." Briefly, this approach entails, the uncritical acceptance of others' beliefs and standards without assimilating them into one's own personality.

Shortly following, the river assisted The Tiger to identify that a major environmental stressor, situation, and or circumstance is when he thinks that various health challenges cannot be resolved; and his quality of health cannot be improved upon.

Then, The Tiger positively stated that he has plans not to argue with his wife anymore, as he wants to have less stress in his life. Furthermore, the river continued and assisted The

Tiger to implement a relaxing thought about how he can improve his quality of health, by pondering about the good health experiencing he had in the past; and how he will have future good health experiencing as well.

THE TIGER

EPISODE FOUR

DIFFERENT AGENCIES IN LOCAL COMMUNITIES CAN HELP WITH THE ACHIEVEMENTS OF PERSONAL GOALS

Mainly, The Tiger has great concerns about his children, as all five of them are current in foster care. Accordingly, The Tiger finds it difficult to eat and maintain sleep throughout the night due to his current distressing experiencing.

For this reason, the river ensured that The Tiger's recovery emerged from hope, by utilizing a reality therapy concept, titled, psychological need for power. In short, this approach entails, the needs for belonging, power, freedom, and fun; these are the forces that drive humans (and in this case The Tiger); and explain behavior.

Immediately following, the river assisted The Tiger to identify that a major environmental stressor, situation, and or circumstance is when he thinks that empowerment cannot be gained when he must accept the help he needs. Indeed, the river further assisted The Tiger to incorporate a distinct plan of action to increase his understanding in this regard, by asking The Tiger to be mindful to have motivational and encouraging thoughts about how when he accepts help from persons from various agencies, he will gain more insight into how to improve his overall behavioral tendencies, in terms of improving his parenting skills and interpersonal relationship skills even more.

Thereafter, The Tiger remarked that he does not want his children in foster care and has decided to receive the necessary help to achieve this very important endeavor.

THE TIGER

EPISODE FIVE

ACHIEVING GOALS REQUIRE CONSTANT TRYING

Today The Tiger presented with a moderate amount of agitation and overall discouragement in his speech; and attitude as well. Namely, The Tiger wants to accomplish his goals of: obtaining his own apartment, getting a car, and working part-time; but he feels that he needs more time to accomplish these, as he is not fully confident that he is ready to be so independent.

Indeed, the river ensured that The Tiger's recovery emerged from respect by utilizing a gestalt therapy concept, titled "confrontation." Basically, this approach entails, an invitation for The Tiger to become aware of discrepancies between verbal and nonverbal expressions, between feelings and actions, or between thoughts and feelings.

Shortly following, the river instructed The Tiger to identify that a major psychosocial stressor for him is when he is not persistent and address his goals in a timely manner to achieve the success he desires. Then, The Tiger stated that he has plans to resume his driving classes with a driving instructor when he is financially able to do so in a few months.

Moreover, the river continued and supported The Tiger to further implement a relaxing thought about how when wanting to learn; and obtain somethings, it takes frequent trying; and that achieving all his goals will require constant trying for many days.

THE TIGER

EPISODE SIX

WRITING APOLOGY LETTERS
TO MAKE MATTERS BETTER

The Tiger presented with an excessive amount of irritation and anger in his mood; and speech as well. Mainly, The Tiger is getting upset frequently and wants to throw things. In fact, The Tiger threw his mother's telephone, and broke it. This, as The Tiger does not believe that his mother is taking care of him in a manner that pleases him; and he wants to inform his mother that he believes that his father is doing more for him than she does. Additionally, The Tiger's mother presented and extensively reported how The Tiger is more appreciative and respectful toward his father, and that his father does not deserves such honor.

Moreover, the river ensured that The Tiger's recovery occurred in a person-driven manner, by utilizing a reality therapy concept/technique/intervention titled "psychological need" pertaining to belonging. In short, this approach entails the needs for belonging, power, freedom, and fun; these are the forces that drive humans and explain behavior.

At length, the river assisted The Tiger to identify that a major environmental stressor, situation, and or circumstance is when he ponders extensively about how his parents are not living in the same home, which result in feelings of resentment for him in many ways.

Furthermore, The Tiger reported that he wants to be more understanding of his mother's sadness, as he does not know why she gets so upset about so many things. Finally, the river continued and supported The Tiger to enact a compliance thought about how since he lost his telephone and tablet usage, due to damaging his mother's phone, this will give him more time to write an apology letter to his mother, to which The Tiger agreed.

THE TIGER

EPISODE SEVEN

ROUTINES ARE IMPORTANT TO DEVELOP SMARTNESS THROUGHOUT LIFE

When presenting today, The Tiger displayed an excessive amount of anxiousness; and overall irritability. Simply speaking, The Tiger's mother presented and extensively reported that The Tiger engages in prolonged watching of U-Tube videos involving the game "Fort Night," as it relates to tournaments. To add, The Tiger does not want to read, and this is a tremendous disappointment for The Tiger's mother, as she reported that The Tiger used to love reading.

For this reason, the river ensured that The Tiger's recovery involves, family, and community strengths, and responsibility, by utilizing a reality therapy concept, titled "cycle of counseling." In short, this approach consists of specific ways of creating a positive climate in which counseling can occur. The proper environment is based on personal involvement and specific procedures aimed at change.

Immediately thereafter, the river assisted The Tiger to identify that a major environmental stressor; and or situation is when he does not develop an increased pattern of behaving to include more activities, such as reading and writing. At length, the river provided The Tiger with a chance to incorporate a distinct plan of change which involves resume attending his football practices in a timely manner so that he can have more things to do with his time.

To this end, the river further instructed The Tiger to implement a relaxing thought about how routines are important to develop to maintain patterns of behaving that will offer smartness throughout his life.

AUTHOR'S BIO

Hi, hello, and how are you, my BLESSED READERS?!
I am your mental wellness counselor: Arlene Williams.

Now, I have prayed; and I believe that God wants me to use
the education that he has given me to help myself and others
obtain a higher level of mental wellness.
In short, I have a master's level of education in
Psychology/ Mental Health Counseling since 2013.
It is safe to say that we will all become physically ill and need
medical attention. Moreover, the same holds that everyone
will develop a mental health condition; and need some
treatment to become mentally well again. Therefore, please
allow us to take a journey into mental wellness living. This,
as you read and apply the key points in the wellness tales
given to me by the SPIRIT of God.

REFERENCE/CITATIONS

Corey, G. (2017). *Student manual for theory and practice of counseling and psychotherapy*. Eight Edition.

CONTACT INFORMATION

TELEPHONE: 407-556-4316

EMAIL: ae270@mynsu.nova.edu

SOCIAL MEDIA INFORMATION:

FACEBOOK @ Arlene Williams

TWITTER @ Arlenew05

Instagram @ Arlene.w28

www.ingramcontent.com/pod-product-compliance
Lightning Source LLC
Chambersburg PA
CBHW071141280326
41935CB00010B/1319